Opening and closing loops and jump rings

1 Hold the loop or jump ring with two pairs of chainnose pliers or chainnose and roundnose pliers, as shown.

2 To open the loop or jump ring, bring the tips of one pair of pliers toward you and push the tips of the other pair away. Reverse the steps to close the open loop or jump ring.

Folded crimp

1 Position the crimp bead in the notch closest to the crimping pliers' handle.
2 Separate the wires and firmly squeeze the crimp.

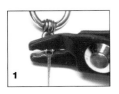

3 Move the crimp into the notch at the pliers' tip and hold the crimp as shown. Squeeze the crimp bead, folding it in half at the indentation.
4 Test that the folded crimp is secure.

Loop

1 Trim the wire or head pin ⅜ in. (1cm) above the top bead. Make a right-angle bend close to the bead.
2 Grab the wire's tip with roundnose pliers. Roll the wire to form a half circle. Release the wire.

3 Reposition the pliers in the loop and continue rolling.
4 The finished loop should form a centered circle above the bead.

Wrapped loop

1 Make sure you have at least 1¼ in. (3.2cm) of wire above the bead. With the tip of your chainnose pliers, grasp the wire directly above the bead. Bend the wire (above the pliers) into a right angle.
2 Using roundnose pliers, position the jaws in the bend.

3 Bring the wire over the top jaw of the roundnose pliers.
4 Reposition the pliers' lower jaw snugly into the loop. Curve the wire downward around the bottom of the roundnose pliers. This is the first half of a wrapped loop.

5 Position the chainnose pliers' jaws across the loop.
6 Wrap the wire around the wire stem, covering the stem between the loop and the top of the bead. Trim the excess wire and press the cut end close to the wraps with chainnose pliers.

Wrapping above a top-drilled bead

1 Center a top-drilled bead on a 3-in. (7.6cm) piece of wire. Bend each wire upward to form a squared-off U shape.

2 Cross the wires into an "X" above the bead.
3 Using chainnose pliers, make a small bend in each wire so the ends form a right angle.
4 Wrap the horizontal wire around the vertical wire as in a wrapped loop. Trim the excess wrapping wire.

Tubular peyote stitch

1 String an even number of beads to equal the desired circumference. Tie in a circle, leaving some ease.

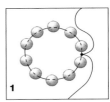

2 Even-numbered beads form row 1 and odd-numbered beads, row 2. (Numbers indicate rows.) Put the ring over a form if desired. Go through the first bead to the left of the knot. Pick up a bead (#1 of row 3), skip a bead, and go through the next bead. Repeat around until you're back to the start.

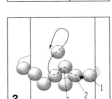

3 Since you started with an even number of beads, you need to work a step up to be in position for the next round. Go through the first beads on rounds 2 and 3. Pick up a bead and go through the second bead of round 3; continue. (If you begin with an odd number of beads, there won't be a step up; you'll keep spiraling.)

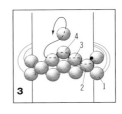

Swinging loops

Add a stylish accent to your wardrobe with easy, playful gemstone earrings. They're surprisingly simple to assemble using beading wire and crimps.

Red and yellow earrings

[1] Cut two 5-in. (13cm) pieces of beading wire.

[2] On each wire, string two rondelles, a spacer, a color B briolette, a spacer, two rondelles, a spacer, a color A briolette, a spacer, two rondelles, a spacer, a B, a spacer, and two rondelles (**photo a**).

[3] Hold the ends of one wire together and string a crimp bead over them. Slide the crimp down toward the beads until the earring is the desired size. Use a pen to mark the crimp's placement (**photo b**). Remove the crimp and mark the second wire to match the first.

[4] String the crimp bead again, then string the earring wire's loop (**photo c**). Take the ends back through the crimp bead, making a small loop around the earring wire (**photo d**). Crimp the crimp bead (see Basics, p. 2) and trim the excess wire close to the crimp.

[5] Hold the crimp cover in the round opening at the tip of your crimping pliers with the crimp's opening facing away from the pliers. Place the cover over the crimp bead (**photo e**).
Gently squeeze the crimping pliers to close the cover over the crimp bead.

[6] Finish the second earring to match the first.

Purple and blue earrings

[1] Begin as in steps 1–2, at left. Tape one end of each wire.

[2] String a crimp bead on the untaped end of one wire. Go through the loop on the earring post and crimp bead (**photo f**). Crimp the crimp bead and trim the excess wire.

[3] Remove the tape, string a crimp bead on the other end of the beading wire, and go through a loop on the earring back. Then go through the crimp bead again (**photo g**). Adjust the beading wire until the earring is the desired length and crimp the crimp bead. Trim the excess wire.

[4] Cover the front crimp bead with a crimp cover as in step 5, at left.

[5] Finish the second earring to match the first.
–*Mel McCabe and Claudia Navarette*
Contact Mel and Claudia at The Bead Shop: (650) 327-0900 or beadshop.com.

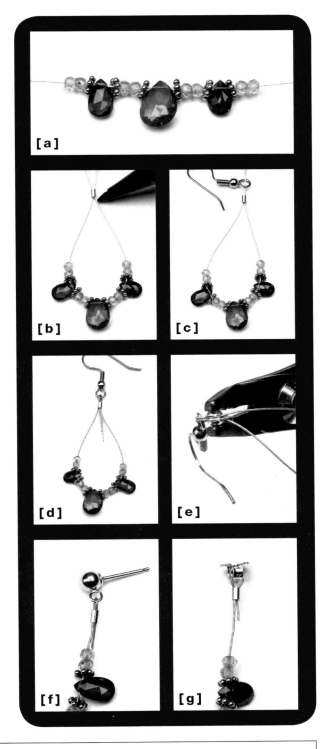

[a]

[b]

[c]

[d]

[e]

[f]

[g]

MATERIALS

both projects
- flexible beading wire, .012–.014, gold or sterling silver finish
- crimping pliers
- wire cutters

red and yellow earrings
- 8mm gemstone briolettes
  2 color A
  4 color B
- **16** 3–4mm faceted gemstone rondelles
- **12** 3–4mm daisy spacers
- **2** medium-size crimp beads

- **2** 3mm crimp covers
- **2** french hook earring wires

purple and blue earrings
- 8mm gemstone briolettes
  2 color A
  4 color B

- **16** 3–4mm faceted gemstone rondelles
- **12** 3–4mm daisy spacers
- **4** crimp beads
- **2** 3mm crimp covers
- **2** post earring findings with loops
- **2** earring backs

Diamond drops

Combine crystal bicones, wire, and chain for a pair of sparkling earrings that will look fabulous with everything from jeans to a cocktail dress.

Dangles

[1] Cut two 3-in. (7.6cm) pieces of wire. Cut two pieces of chain with three attached links each.

[2] Slide a teardrop crystal to 1 in. (2.5cm) from the end of a 3-in. length of wire. Bend the wire ends up next to the point of the crystal and cross the wires above it (**photo a**). Make two wraps with the short end of the wire and trim the excess (**photo b**). Flatten the end of the wire against the wraps with chainnose pliers.

[3] Make a 90-degree bend ⅛ in. (3mm) from the first set of wraps and start a wrapped loop (**photo c** and

Basics, p. 2). Slide an end link of one three-link chain into the loop and finish with two wraps (**photo d**). Cut off any excess wire and flatten the end with chainnose pliers.

[4] Repeat to make a second dangle and set both aside.

Hoop

[1] Cut two 8-in. (20cm) pieces of wire. Make a wrapped loop at the end of one 8-in. length of wire. String a spacer, a 4mm crystal, and a spacer. Bend the wire at a 45-degree angle ⅛ in. (3mm) away from the last spacer (**photo e**).

[2] String eight 4mm crystals on the

wire. Make a 90-degree bend with your fingers just past the last crystal (**photo f**).

[3] Repeat step 2 three more times (**photo g**).

[4] String a chain dangle on the wire. Wrap the wire end twice under the spacer (**photo h**).

[5] Trim any excess wire and flatten the end with chainnose pliers.

[6] Make a second earring to match. Open the loop (Basics) on each earring finding and attach a hoop. Close the loops.

–Molli Schultz
Contact Molli at
wheresmolli@yahoo.com.

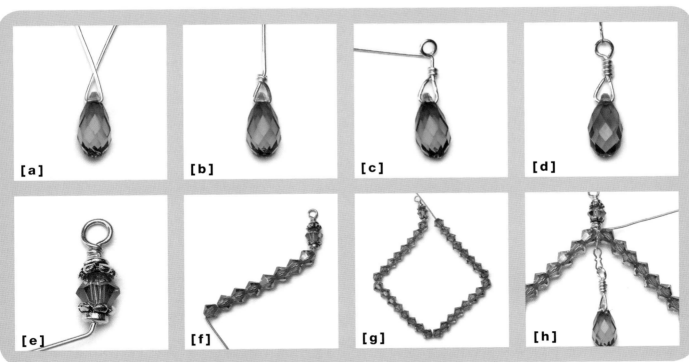

[a] [b] [c] [d]

[e] [f] [g] [h]

MATERIALS

one pair of earrings

- **66** 4mm bicone crystals
- **2** 5 x 7mm top-drilled teardrop crystals
- **4** 3mm spacers
- **7** links or 1½ in. (3.8cm) of fine chain
- **22** in. (56cm) 22- or 24-gauge wire
- **2** earring findings
- chainnose pliers
- roundnose pliers
- wire cutters

EDITOR'S NOTE:

Make a smaller earring by reducing the number of crystals strung in step 2 of the hoop and attaching a shorter dangle.

Creative clusters

If you want maximum wear from a few basic earring styles, consider this modular approach. The bead clusters shown on the hoop earrings employ an extended version of wrapped loops; the pearl clusters use chain instead of wraps.

MATERIALS

leaf clusters
- 8 Czech glass leaves
- 8 5mm faceted quartz crystal buttons
- 3½ ft. (1m) 24-gauge, half-hard silver wire
- 2 6mm split rings

tanzanite clusters
- 8 7mm faceted tanzanite buttons
- 8 5mm faceted quartz crystal buttons
- 8 4-in. (10cm) ultra-fine head pins
- 2 6mm split rings
- 2 hoop earrings, 3mm tubing

pearl clusters
- 14 3–5mm pearls, one or more colors, or a mix of pearls and crystals
- 14 4-in. ultra-fine head pins or 5 ft. (1.4m) 24-gauge half-hard wire
- 12 in. (30cm) chain
- 2 6mm split rings
- pair earring findings

all projects
- chainnose pliers
- roundnose pliers
- split-ring pliers
- wire cutters
- file (optional)
- hammer (optional)

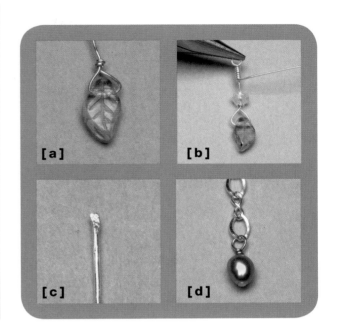

[a]   [b]   [c]   [d]

Leaf clusters

[1] Cut eight 5-in. (13cm) pieces of wire. String a glass leaf ¾ in. (1.9cm) from the end of one piece. Make a wrapped loop above the leaf (see Basics, p. 2 and **photo a**). String a crystal onto the wire.

[2] Using chainnose pliers, bend the wire into a right angle about ⅜ in. (1cm) above the crystal to start the wrapped loop (Basics). Vary this length slightly when you make the other leaf dangles. Make the first half of a small wrapped loop.

[3] Hold the loop with pliers and continue to wrap the stem (**photo b**). Keep the coils close together and uniform and wrap the entire stem from loop to crystal. Trim the wire close to the last wrap. Make eight dangles.

[4] Open one split ring and slide four dangles into place. Slide the four remaining dangles on another split ring.

Tanzanite clusters

[1] Use eight head pins or cut eight 4-in. (10cm) pieces of wire. If you're using wire, create a "head" in one of two ways: Flatten the wire tip with a hammer, trim the flat section with wire cutters, then file until smooth (**photo c**). Or, make a tiny loop at one end of the wire and pinch it closed with pliers.

[2] String a tanzanite and a crystal onto the wire. Start a wrapped loop above the beads, wrapping the stem as in step 3 of the leaf dangles. Make eight dangles.

[3] Open a split ring and slide four dangles into place. Slide the remaining four dangles onto another split ring.

Pearl clusters

[1] String a pearl onto a head pin, as in the tanzanite clusters. Make the first half of a wrapped loop.

[2] Insert the end link of chain into the loop. Complete the wraps (**photo d**).

[3] Cut the chain to the desired length for each dangle. Open the split ring and insert the end link.

[4] Make 14 dangles and divide them evenly between the two split rings.
–*Mindy Brooks*
Mindy is Editor of Bead&Button *magazine.*

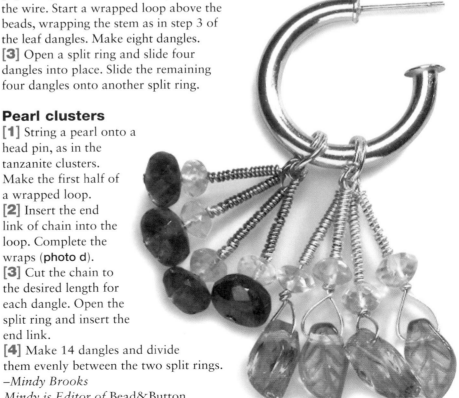

Vintage style

These earrings are reminiscent of the vintage style popular in the late sixties and early seventies. Use different accent, art, and enamel beads to make each pair original.

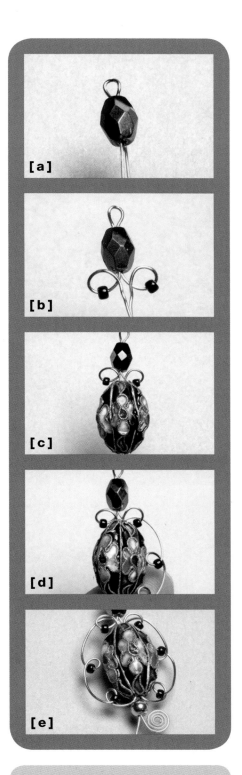

[a]

[b]

[c]

[d]

[e]

[1] Bend an 8-in. (20cm) length of wire in half. Insert the cut ends into the smaller of the two decorative beads, leaving a ⅜-in. (1cm) loop above the bead (**photo a**).

[2] String a seed bead onto one of the wire ends. Make a small, round loop right below the decorative bead and slide the seed bead into the loop. Repeat with the other wire. The loops should be oriented as mirror images of each other (**photo b**).

[3] String the larger decorative bead onto both wires (**photo c**).

[4] With one wire, make a round loop close to the bottom of the decorative bead, string a seed bead, and slide it into the loop. Make another loop halfway up the side and add a seed bead as before.

[5] Thread the wire through the loop made in step 2 and back through the large bead (**photo d**).

[6] Working with the second wire, repeat steps 4 and 5 on the opposite side of the bead. Threading this wire through the large bead can take several attempts, so be patient.

[7] String a 3mm bead onto both wires. Trim the wires to 1½ in. (3.8cm) and

roll each wire into a tight coil to finish the ends (**photo e**).

[8] Open the loop (see Basics, p. 2) on the earwire and attach the loop above the smaller decorative bead.

[9] Make the second earring to match the first.

–Wendy Witchner

Wendy is a frequent contributor to Bead&Button *and* BeadStyle *magazines.*

MATERIALS

both pairs of earrings
- **2** 3mm round beads
- **12** seed beads, size 11º
- **2** earring wires
- **1** yd. (.9m) 24-gauge craft wire
- roundnose pliers
- wire cutters

tall earrings
- **2** 19 x 11mm oval beads
- **2** 6mm bicone or round beads

short earrings
- **2** 8mm round faceted fire-polished crystals
- **2** 8 x 12mm beads

EDITOR'S NOTE: Try bending the wire by hand, instead of using pliers.

Sparkling chandeliers

Use chain to make dramatic chandelier earrings with length and movement. These fun earrings may look complicated, but all you need are a few basic techniques.

Blue and silver earrings

[1] Cut two three-link pieces of 1.25mm chain, two nine-link pieces, and one 11-link piece.

[2] Cut a 2-in. (5cm) length of 24-gauge wire. Make the first half of a wrapped loop (see Basics, p. 2). Attach the loop to a soldered jump ring (**photo a**) and complete the wrap.

[3] String a color A 4mm crystal on the wire against the wrap. Make the first half of a wrapped loop above the crystal and in the same plane as the first loop. Attach the end link of a three-link piece of chain (**photo b**). Finish the wrap.

[4] Cut a 2-in. length of 24-gauge wire and make the first half of a wrapped loop. Attach the other end link of the chain from the previous step and finish the wrap.

[5] String a color B crystal on the wire and make the first half of a wrapped loop. Attach the end links of a nine-link piece of chain and the 11-link chain (**photo c**). Complete the wraps.

[6] Repeat steps 2–5 to attach the remaining chains from step 1 to the other side of the soldered jump ring and the long crossing chain (**photo d**). Make sure the crossing chain is not twisted before attaching it to the second side.

[7] Make the end dangles by stringing a color A crystal on a head pin and making a wrapped loop. Make two.

[8] For the remaining dangles, make a head pin unit with a crystal, as in step 7, but attach a length of chain before completing the wraps. The crystal colors will alternate and the chain lengths will differ as follows:
• Color B crystal, two chain links (make two)
• C, four links (make two)
• B, six links (make two)
• C, eight links (make two)
• A, ten links (make one)

[9] Cut a 2-in. piece of 22-gauge wire and make a loop at one end (Basics).

[10] Start with an end dangle and string one dangle from each set, in graduated order, placing a 3mm crystal between each dangle. String the remaining dangles as a mirror image of the first half (**photo e**).

[11] Trim the wire to ⅜ in. (1cm) past the last dangle and make a loop in the same plane as the first (**photo f**).

[12] Attach an end link of chain from step 6 to each loop (**photo g**) and close the loops tightly.

[13] String a color B crystal on a head pin and start a wrapped loop. Slide the loop through the middle link on the crossing chain (**photo h**) and complete the wraps. Skip a link and attach a 3mm crystal on each side of the center dangle.

[14] Open the loop on the earring finding and attach it to the soldered jump ring.

[15] Make the second earring to match the first.

Fire-polished and gold earrings

The fire-polished earrings follow the same basic instructions as the blue and silver earrings, but use a chain with larger links (2.5mm) and one color of fire-polished beads instead of three colors of 4mm crystals. Follow the instructions above, with the following changes:

In step 1, cut two two-link pieces, two seven-link pieces, and one nine-link piece of chain. Where the instructions above call for the three-link chain, use the two-link chain, and substitute the seven- and nine-link chains for the nine- and eleven-link chains.

In step 8, use the following pattern to make the dangles with the 2.5mm chain:
• bead, one link (make two)
• bead, two links (make two)
• bead, three links (make two)
• bead, four links (make two)
• bead, five links (make one)
In step 13, don't skip links when attaching dangles to the long linking chain.

AB crystal earrings

[1] Cut three 13-link and one 27-link pieces of chain.

[2] Follow step 2 for the blue and silver earrings. String a 4mm crystal and start a wrapped loop. Attach the end link of two 13-link pieces of chain and complete the wraps.

[3] Make another crystal unit and attach one loop to the jump ring. Attach the other loop to the remaining 13-link chain and the closest end link on the chain from the previous step. Don't twist the crossing chain.

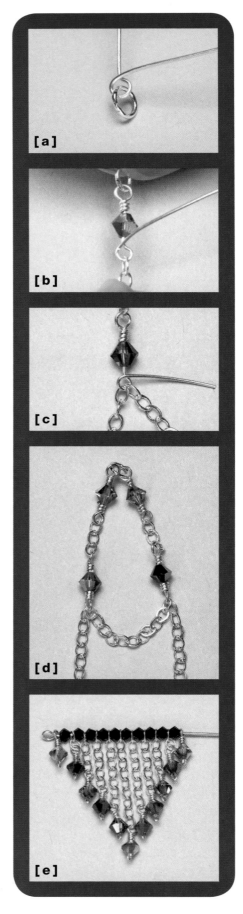

[4] Cut a 2-in. piece of 22-gauge wire and make a loop at one end. Slide an end link on the 27-link chain on the wire and string a 6 x 12mm, 6mm, and 6 x 12mm crystal. Go through the other end link on the long chain and make another loop in the same plane as the first.

[f]

[g]

[h]

[5] String an 8mm crystal on a head pin and start a wrapped loop. Attach the loop to the middle link of the 27-link chain and complete the wrap. Then add the following crystal dangles to each side of the 8mm:
• skip three links; attach a 6mm crystal
• skip a link; attach a 4mm crystal
• skip a link; attach a 4mm crystal
[6] Make a 6mm dangle and hang it from the middle link of the crossing chain.
[7] Attach the earring finding.
[8] Make the second earring to match the first.

Bone bead earrings

Follow the instructions for the AB crystal earrings with the changes listed below, and refer to the picture of the bone earring to determine the placement of each bead color.

In steps 2 and 3, the bead units are attached to the end loops on the finding instead of to a jump ring.

In step 4, attach the chain between the middle and end beads. The length of the middle bead will determine the length of chain (this one has 23 links).

In step 5, make five bead dangles and attach the first one to the middle link of chain. Add two dangles to each side: skip one link, add a dangle, skip two links, and add a dangle.

In step 7, attach a dangle to the middle loop on the finding.
–Melody MacDuffee
Contact Melody at (251) 342-9076 or writersink@msn.com.

EDITOR'S NOTE: To cut multiple pieces of chain the same length, cut the first piece to the desired length, slide the end link on a wire, and string the end link of the remaining chain on the wire next to the cut piece. Hold the wire so both chains hang freely and cut the second piece to match the first.

MATERIALS

blue and silver earrings
• Swarovski bicone crystals
   10 4mm, color A
   14 4mm, color B
   8 4mm, color C
   24 3mm
• 18 in. (46cm) 1.25mm chain
• 4 in. (10cm) 22-gauge wire
• 16 in. (41cm) 24-gauge wire
• 28 head pins
• 2 post earring findings
• 2 4-6mm soldered jump rings

fire-polished and gold earrings
• 32 4mm Czech fire-polished beads
• 24 3mm Swarovski bicone crystals
• 18 in. (46cm) chain, 2.5mm
• 4 in. (10cm) 22-gauge wire
• 16 in. (41cm) 24-gauge wire
• 28 head pins
• 2 earring findings

AB crystal earrings
• Swarovski bicone crystals
   12 4mm
   2 8mm
   8 6mm
   4 6 x 12mm
• 12 in. (30cm) chain, 1.25mm
• 4 in. (10cm) 22-gauge wire
• 8 in. (20cm) 24-gauge wire
• 16 head pins
• 2 4-6mm soldered jump rings
• 2 post earring findings

Bone bead earrings
• 4mm round beads
   10 turquoise
   12 tiger eye
• 2 10 x 20mm bone beads
• 12 in. (30cm) chain, 1.25mm
• 4 in. (10cm) 22-gauge wire
• 8 in. (20cm) 24-gauge wire
• 14 head pins
• 2 3-to-1 findings
• 2 earring findings

all projects
• roundnose pliers
• chainnose pliers
• wire cutters

Golden dangles

Create elegant dangle earrings with the rich glow of gold. These eye-catching dangles are sophisticated and dramatic, yet easy to assemble.

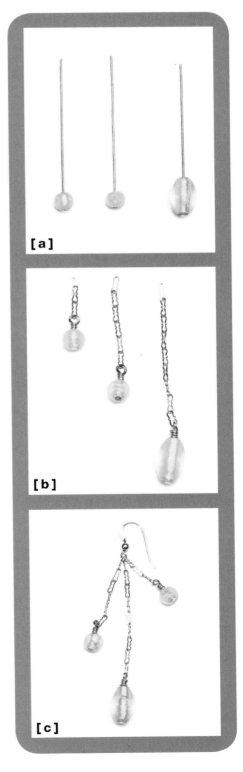

[a]

[b]

[c]

[1] String two 6mm round beads and one 8 x 12mm bead on head pins (**photo a**). Start a wrapped loop (see Basics, p. 2) above each bead.

[2] Cut a three-link piece of chain, a six-link piece of chain, and a nine-link piece of chain. Attach each of the shorter chains to one of the 6mm bead units, and attach the longest chain to the 8 x 12mm bead unit. Finish the wraps (**photo b**).

[3] Open the loop (Basics) on the earring finding and attach the end link of each chain, with the longest chain in the middle (**photo c**). Close the loop.

[4] Make the second earring to match the first.

–Lesley Weiss

Lesley is Assistant Editor at Kalmbach Books.

MATERIALS

pair of earrings

- **4** 6mm round gold foil beads, frosted
- **2** 8 x 12mm oval gold foil beads, frosted
- 8 in. (20cm) flat crinkle chain
- **6** 2-in. (5cm) gold-filled head pins
- pair of earring findings
- chainnose pliers
- roundnose pliers
- wire cutters

Window earrings

These fun seed bead earrings have an element of surprise in the window.

Peyote circle

[1] Thread a needle with 1 yd. (.9m) of Fireline. Pick up an even number of color A beads, enough to encircle your focal bead (**photo a**). Tie them into a circle using a surgeon's knot (see Basics, p. 2).

[2] Working in circular peyote (Basics), stitch around the ring. When you return to the first bead in the circle, step up to the next row (Basics and **photo b**). Stitch one more row.

[3] To work the fifth and final row, pick up two color B beads as you make each stitch as in **photo c**.

Bail

[1] When you reach the last space in the outermost row, pick up six Bs to make the bail. Go through the first bead in the last row of the ring (**photo d**). Do not cut the thread.

[2] Weave down through the beads and exit the first row directly underneath the bail (**photo e**).

Dangle

[1] Pick up two Bs, the focal bead, and one B.

[2] Go back through the focal bead and pick up two Bs. Go through the

adjacent bead in the first row and weave through several nearby beads (**photo f**).

[3] Tie off your thread using half-hitch knots (Basics) and trim the tails.

[4] Open the loop on an earring finding, attach the bail, and close the loop.

[5] Make a second earring to match the first.

Variations

In the photo above, the focal beads and the accent beads around the perimeter are pearls. Other options include using small gemstones, nuggets, or stone chips as focal beads. In **photo g**, I used 5º hex beads around the perimeter. In **photo h**, the 6ºs along the beaded edging add drama to the dangling green crystal.

For a more fanciful look, try using bugle beads around the edge as in **photo i**. Pick up a bugle and 15º, then go through the bugle and the nearest bead in the row and continue around. If your bugles aren't large enough, add a 15º on either side to fill in the gaps.

–Fran Morris Mandel
Contact Fran through
uky.edu/socialwork/www or at
franvmorris@yahoo.com.

MATERIALS

- seed beads, size 11º
  5g color A
  2g color B
- **2** medium-weight focal beads
- variety of beads for embellishment (optional)
- Fireline, 6 lb. test
- beading needles, #12
- pair of earring findings
- flatnose pliers

EDITOR'S NOTE: When working in circular peyote, your edges may start to curl up. Using a little less tension in your stitches can help keep your work flat.

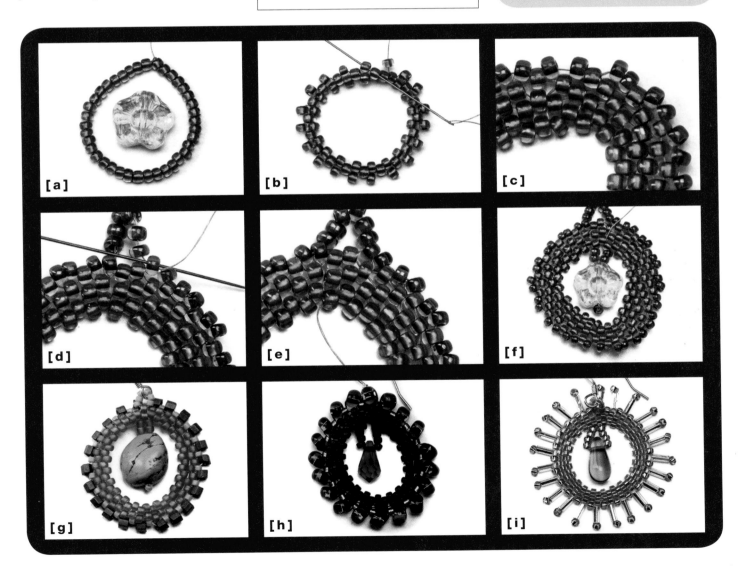

[a]
[b]
[c]
[d]
[e]
[f]
[g]
[h]
[i]

Beaded blossoms

Beautiful flower earrings can be simple textured balls or fully-blooming dangles. Embellish as you like.

Variation 3 – open center

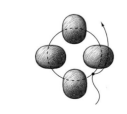

Variation 2 – double petals

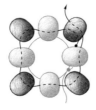

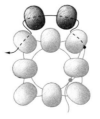

Sunflower dangles

MATERIALS

beaded ball earrings
- 2g Charlottes, size 13º
- 2-in. (5cm) corsage pins or post earrings with 6mm balls
- earring backs or nuts

earrings with petal variations
- 2g Charlottes, size 13º
- **16–32** 2–3mm rice-shaped freshwater pearls
- 2-in. (5cm) corsage pins or post earrings with 6mm balls

sunflower dangle earrings
- 2–3g Charlottes, size 13º
- **40** 2 or 3mm rice-shaped freshwater pearls
- **2** 6mm round beads or corsage pins
- earring wires with loop

star earrings
- 2g size 11º seed beads
- **20** 2–3mm rice-shaped freshwater pearls
- **2** 3mm round freshwater pearls or beads
- post earrings with 8mm pad

all earrings
- Nymo B
- beeswax or Thread Heaven
- beading needles, #13 or smaller
- cyanoacrylate glue
- wire cutters
- metal file (optional)

Beaded ball earrings

Row 1: String four Charlottes onto a yard (.9m) of waxed thread, leaving a 4-in. (10cm) tail. Tie the beads into a circle using a surgeon's knot (see Basics, p. 2). Continue through the first bead in the ring (**figure 1**). Insert the earring post or the corsage pin shaft into the circle of beads, so the beads rest against the ball.

Row 2: To begin covering the ball in peyote stitch (Basics), string a Charlotte and go through the next bead in the circle. Repeat three more times. Go through the first bead in row 1 and step up through the first bead in row 2 (**figure 2**).

Row 3: String two Charlottes and go through the next bead in row 2 (**figure 3**). Repeat three more times (eight beads total). Step up through the first bead in row 3.

Row 4: String a Charlotte and go through the next Charlotte. Continue around the circle, adding one bead in each space and one between each pair added in row 3 (eight beads total). Step up to the next row as before.

Rows 5–7: Work even-count peyote around the circle, stepping up before starting each new row. When you've completed row 7, thread a needle on the thread tail at the start of the beadwork. Secure the thread in the beads and trim it. Slide the beads away from the ball. Using the tip of a needle or other fine applicator, dot the ball with glue where the ball meets the pin or post. Press the beads against the glued ball. Don't allow the glue to show or fill the bead holes. Let the earring dry completely.

Rows 8–10: Work even-count peyote around the circle, stepping up before starting each new row.

Row 11: String a Charlotte and go through the next two Charlottes. Repeat around the circle (four beads total) (**figure 4**). Step up to the next row.

FIGURE 1   **FIGURE 2**   **FIGURE 3**   **FIGURE 4**